W9-BEA-617

DISCARD

MUSICAL
INSTRUMENTS
OF THE WORLD

Flutes

Barrie Carson Turner

Illustrated by John See

Smart Apple Media

PEIRCE SCHOOL LIBRARY
1423 W. BRYN MAWR AVE.
CHICAGO, IL. 60660
773-534-2440

First published in the UK in 1998 by
Belitha Press Limited
London House, Great Eastern Wharf,
Parkgate Road, London SW11 4NQ

Text by Barrie Carson Turner   Illustrations by John See
Text and illustrations copyright © Belitha Press Ltd 1998
Cover design by The Design Lab

Published in the United States by
Smart Apple Media
123 South Broad Street
Mankato, Minnesota 56001

Copyright ©1999 Smart Apple Media
International copyright observed in all countries. No part of this book may be
reproduced in any form without written permission from the publisher.

ISBN: 1-887068-45-7

Library of Congress Cataloging-in-Publication Data

Turner, Barrie.
    Flutes / Barrie Carson Turner.
        p.   cm. — (The musical instruments of the world)
    Includes index.
    Summary: Describes eighteen flutes that make up a large part of the woodwind
family, including the piccolo, fife, suling, and nay.
    ISBN 1-887068-45-7
    1. Woodwind instruments—Juvenile literature.   [1. Woodwind instruments.]
I. Title. II. Series.
ML930.T87 1998
788.3' 19—dc21   98-6279

Printed in Hong Kong / China

9   8   7   6   5   4   3   2   1

Picture acknowledgements

James Davis Travel Photography: 27; the Defense Picture Library: 8; Eye Ubiquitous: 23;
Robert Harding Picture Library: 14, 16; The Hutchison Library: 15 Michael MacIntyre;
The Japan Archive: 11; Magnum Photos: 9, 12 Burt Glinn; Performing Arts Library: 13, 21,
28-29 Clive Barda; Redferns: 22 Brian Shuel; Peter Sanders Photography: 26;
Trip: 4-5 P. Rauter. 6-7 G. Horner; Tropix: 25; John Walmsley Photo Library: 18, 19

Contents

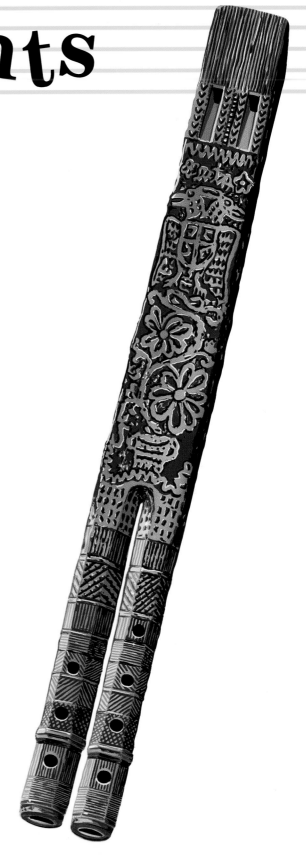

Musical

Musical instruments are played in every country of the world. There are many thousands of different instruments in all shapes and sizes. They are often grouped into four families: strings, brass, percussion, and woodwind.

Brass and woodwind instruments are blown to make their sound. Percussion instruments are struck (hit), shaken, or scraped to make their sound. Stringed instruments make sounds when their strings vibrate.

instruments

This book is about flutes, which are part of the woodwind family. Some flutes, like the piccolo and the suling, are played in orchestras. Others, like the fife, are played in marching bands. You will often hear the sports whistle on the football field.

This book tells us about 18 flutes from all over the world. There is a picture of each instrument and a photograph of a performer playing it.
On pages 30 and 31 you will find a list of useful words to help you understand more about music.

Flute

The flute is an important instrument to the orchestra. Flutes were once made of wood, but today they are usually made of metal or even gold or silver. The mouthpiece is at one end of the instrument, where the metal is shaped to make a resting place for the lips. The musician blows across (not into) the blow hole. Each finger hole is covered by a small metal cap called a key.

key

foot joint

lip plate

blow hole

head joint

middle joint

The player makes different notes by pressing down on the keys. The flute is built in three sections called joints so that the instrument can be taken apart and carried easily. Flute players are called flautists.

The flute often plays the tune in a piece of music. A flute's low notes are rich and mellow. Its high notes are bright and powerful.

Bosun's pipe

mouthpiece

This tiny metal pipe is just a little over 1 1/4 inches (10 cm) long. The player blows into the mouthpiece. The air rushes through the pipe and hits the edge of a small hole, creating a loud whistling sound. The player holds the bosun's pipe in one hand. He opens or closes his hand to make different sounds.

carrying ring

The bosun's pipe is played by sailors. They blow it to welcome important people on board a ship.

hole

Di

The di (ti) has been played in China for more than a thousand years. The instrument is made from bamboo and is blown through a hole near one end. A thin piece of tissue paper is pasted over one of its holes. When the flute is blown, the paper adds a buzzing sound.

blow hole

bamboo tube

tissue paper

finger hole

In ancient times, the di was often carved with a dragon's head at one end and a tail at the other end. Today, the di usually has no decoration.

Shakuhachi

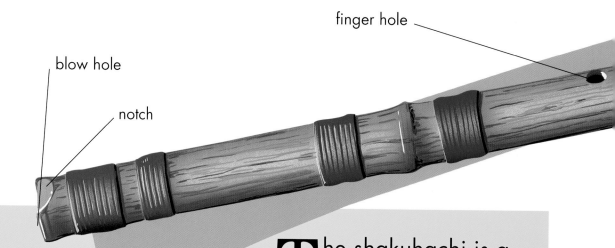

blow hole

notch

finger hole

The shakuhachi is a Japanese flute and is traditionally played by men. It is made from bamboo, which is cut near the bottom of the plant where the stem becomes wider. This construction gives the instrument its curved shape. The player rests the instrument on his lower lip and blows against a small notch cut into the side of the tube. The shakuhachi makes a beautiful, clear sound.

At one time the shakuhachi was played by priests, who also used the instrument as a weapon of self-defense. The instrument is still popular in Japan today and is played in classical and folk music.

In the past, shakuhachi players had to wear baskets over their heads so that no one could recognize them. Today players still wear baskets over their heads when they play.

11

Fife

The fife is usually made of wood. The fife is held in the same way as the flute, out to the side of the player. The instrument has a high shrill sound. The player makes different notes by covering the finger holes. The finger holes on some fifes are covered by metal caps called keys.

blow hole

lip plate

finger hole

Today the fife is often played in marching bands. The bands play the same music that soldiers marched to hundreds of years ago.

12

Piccolo

The piccolo is a small flute. It is made of wood, metal, or a combination of both. It plays the highest notes in the orchestra and makes a loud sound that can be heard above all the other instruments. Small metal caps called keys cover the finger holes. The player makes different notes by pressing down on the keys.

blow hole

key

The piccolo is held and played like the flute. *Piccolo* is an Italian word that means "small."

Nose flute

Nose flutes are usually played from the top, like the recorder. They are held against the nose and blown through one nostril, while the thumb holds the other nostril closed. In some countries, people believe that breath blown from the nose is magical, so the nose flute is often played at religious ceremonies.

finger hole

This musician is about to play two nose flutes at the same time.

Suling

palm leaf ring

The suling is made from bamboo and comes from Indonesia. The instrument is sometimes called a ring flute, because it has a ring of palm leaves wrapped around the blow hole. The ring of leaves helps to direct the player's breath into the hole. Some players can blow air out and breathe it in at the same time. This is called circular breathing.

finger hole

Sulings are made in different sizes. Sulings are usually played with a group of percussion instruments called a gamelan orchestra.

15

Recorder

Recorders have been played in Europe for hundreds of years. Recorders have a soft tone and must be blown very gently. They sound better played in small groups or as a solo instrument, rather than in an orchestra. There are five instruments in the recorder family. The highest is the sopranino. This is a tiny recorder with finger holes very close together.

crook

These children are playing descant recorders. The descant recorder is the instrument most often played in schools.

family

tenor

treble

descant

finger hole

mouthpiece

sopranino

bass

The descant recorder is the next highest instrument. The treble and tenor are bigger and lower-sounding recorders. The large bass recorder plays very low notes. It is so big that it has an extra metal tube called a crook, which helps the player reach the finger holes.

Swannee whistle

mouthpiece

The swannee whistle has no finger holes. Instead, the different notes are made by a plunger held in the right hand. As the plunger is pushed in, the notes slide higher. As the plunger is pulled out, the notes slide lower. No one knows how the swannee whistle got its name.

plunger

The notes on a swannee whistle slide up and down with a whooping sound. Because of its sound, the swannee whistle is sometimes used in music for funny films.

18

Nightingale

Most flutes are tube-shaped, but the nightingale is shaped like a bird. First the instrument is filled with water. Then the player blows down a spout in the bird's tail. The air bubbles through the water and escapes through a small hole in the bird's head.

air escape hole

beak

blow spout

This nightingale is made of clay. This flute makes a low warbling sound, just like a bird. Plastic nightingales make a higher-pitched whistle.

19

Panpipes

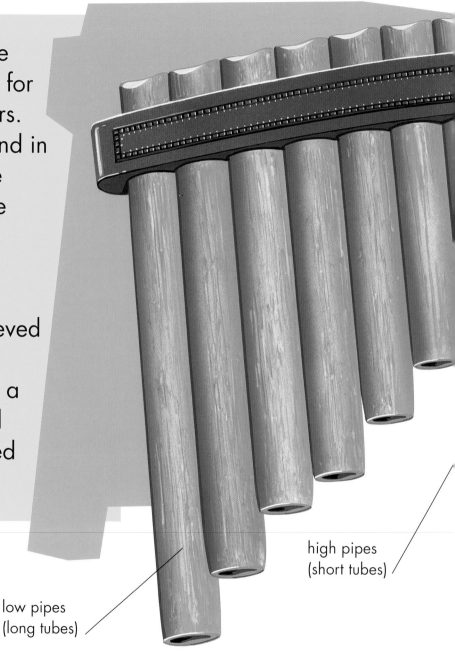

Panpipes have been played for thousands of years. Panpipes are found in many parts of the world and can be made of reed, bamboo, wood, stone, or pottery. People once believed that these pipes were invented by a Greek god called Pan, so they called them panpipes.

high pipes
(short tubes)

low pipes
(long tubes)

Each pipe in a set of panpipes is a tiny flute that plays just one note. The pipes that make up the instrument are of different lengths. The long pipes make low sounds and the short pipes make high sounds. The pipes are tied together in a bundle or made into a raft shape.

This player is from South America, where the panpipes are very popular. Players blow across the tops of the pipes to make a light, reedy sound.

Tin whistle

The tin whistle is much like the recorder, but the tin whistle is made of metal. This whistle has only six finger holes and no thumb hole. In the past, the tin whistle was often played by street musicians. People would give the player a penny, which is why the tin whistle is also called a penny whistle.

The tin whistle has a bright, high-pitched sound and is ideal for playing lively dance tunes, such as reels and jigs.

mouthpiece

finger hole

Sports whistle

The sports whistle is blown through a short, wide tube called a duct. At the other end of the tube, the air hits the sharp edge of a long, narrow hole in the metal body. The whistle makes a loud, shrill sound. A small clay pea inside the whistle adds a warble to the tone.

mouthpiece

duct

narrow hole

carrying ring

The sound of the sports whistle carries a long way, which makes the whistle useful on the playing field. The whistle is also often blown at carnivals and street parties.

Ocarina

Most flutes are shaped like a tube, but the ocarina is usually round or shaped like a long egg. Small ocarinas make high sounds, and large ocarinas make low sounds. Some ocarinas have a tuning plunger. When this is pushed in or pulled out, it makes the instrument sound higher or lower.

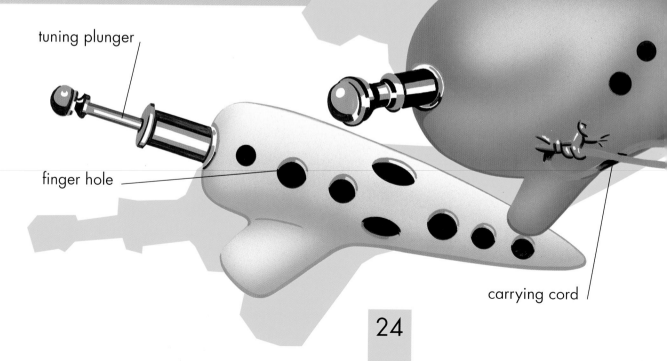

tuning plunger

finger hole

carrying cord

Ocarinas were first played thousands of years ago. At first they were made from bones, large hollow seeds, and other natural objects. Now ocarinas can be made of clay, china, and even plastic. The word *ocarina* is Italian and means "little goose." These flutes were called this because in Italy ocarinas were shaped like a bird.

blow hole

Most ocarinas have at least one finger hole. Players cover and uncover the finger holes to make different notes.

25

Nay

The nay is a very old instrument, played centuries ago in ancient Egypt. Today the nay is still played in Egypt and other nearby countries. The nay is made from bamboo, wood, or metal, and the longest nays are about 3 feet (1m) long. The players make different notes by covering the finger holes and by moving their lips as they blow.

finger hole

The nay rests on the bottom lip. The player blows across the top edge of the instrument to make a soft, reedy tone.

Double flute

The double flute is two instruments in one. Sometimes these two flute pipes are carved from one piece of wood. Sometimes they are bound together. Musicians must be able to breathe deeply, as the instrument takes more breath to play than a single flute.

double mouthpiece

finger hole

separate pipes

Double flute players often play two tunes at the same time—one on each pipe. The flute's sound is soft and bright.

27

Bass flute

Bass flutes are made of metal. The instrument is very heavy and is so long that it has to be wrapped around at one end so that the player can reach all of the finger holes. Each finger hole is covered by a small metal cap called a key.

The bass flute plays very low notes. A bass flute player is called a bass flautist.

Players make different notes by pressing down on the keys. The blow hole has a lip rest, which allows players to rest their lips comfortably as they play. Players blow against the edge of the blow hole, not into it. The bass flute is played in an orchestra, but composers don't write music for this instrument very often.

lip plate

blow hole

key

Words to

bamboo A kind of tall grass with a hard, hollow stem. Bamboo is often used to make musical instruments.

blow hole The hole into which a player blows to play a flute.

body The main part of an instrument.

carnival A festival held outdoors, with music and dancing.

crook An extra piece of tubing on some long instruments that helps the player reach all of the finger holes.

duct The long front part of a flute mouthpiece.

family (of instruments) Instruments that are similar to each other.

finger holes The holes a player covers to make different notes.

flute An instrument usually made in the shape of a tube. It is blown to make a sound.

folk music Popular songs or tunes so old that no one knows who wrote them.

gamelan orchestra An orchestra from Indonesia that is made up of many different instruments.

joint A part of a flute or pipe. The joints fit together to make the whole instrument. A joint is also the point at which the parts join.

key A small metal cap covering a finger hole on a wind instrument.

lip rest A rest for a player's lips that makes it easier to blow into an instrument.

marching band A group of musicians who play military (soldiers') music as they march along.

30

remember

mellow A word used to describe a soft, warm, gentle sound.

musician Someone who plays an instrument or sings.

mouthpiece The part of a wind instrument held in the mouth and blown.

notch A V-shaped cut. A notch at the top of a flute makes it easier to blow.

orchestra A large group of musicians playing together.

performer Someone who plays or sings to other people.

pipe In music, some flutes are also called pipes. A pipe is one of the tubes that makes up the panpipes.

plunger The part of a swannee whistle that is pushed in and pulled out to make different notes.

reedy A word used to describe a low, buzzing sound.

shrill A word used to describe a high, loud sound.

solo A piece of music played or sung by one performer.

street musician A performer who plays in the street for money. A street musician is also called a busker.

tone How an instrument sounds. For instance, an instrument may have a bright tone or a dull tone.

tuning plunger A tube that is pushed in or pulled out of an ocarina to change the notes it can play.

vibrate To move up and down very quickly.

whistle A very high-sounding flute or a very shrill sound.

Index

PEIRCE SCHOOL LIBRARY
1423 W. BRYN MAWR AVE.
CHICAGO, IL. 60660
773-534-2440